# AN URGENT PLEA:

# DO NOT CHANGE THE PAPACY

by

Atila Sinke Guimarães

Michael J. Matt

John Vennari

Marian Therese Horvat, Ph.D.

ISBN: 0-9672166-4-8
Library of Congress Number: 2001117201
Printed and bound in the United States of America

Cover: John Paul II's moment of prayer at the Wailing Wall in Jerusalem (March 26, 2000).

**Tradition In Action, Inc.**
PO Box 23135
Los Angeles, CA  90023

# A WORD TO THE READER

One year after having launched the important document *We Resist You to the Face*, the same four lay journalists have signed a new open letter to Pope John Paul II. Here, also, the title summarizes its message: *An Urgent Plea: Do Not Change the Papacy.*

The change of the Papacy has been announced more or less everywhere. Voices are heard supporting such a change and asking that it be radical. Until now, not a word of significance had come from the conservative or traditionalist milieu. This pole of Catholic thinking expresses itself in this document with admirable boldness, intellectual valor, and distinction.

The authors analyze the plan of John Paul II to change the Petrine Primacy in order to make it acceptable to Schismatics and Protestants. They object to the proposed measures and alleged motives for a change. Confronting the Pope, they ask him not to change the Papacy. It is, without a doubt, a bold request, which startles those who show more consideration for authority than for the Faith. However, the authors demonstrate the simple and unpretentious courage that belongs to those who have dedicated their lives to defend the Catholic Church. They have the innocent audacity of the "little people" – for is it not true that laymen are the least among the members of the Church? Their Catholic Faith is sincere, and clearly they are moved by a duty of conscience. They honestly believe that John Paul II is wrong regarding his planned reform of the Papacy. They have no indecision: they address themselves directly to the Pope. There can be no error in following such a course. Why shouldn't Catholics be able to reverently direct themselves to the Supreme Pontiff on such a serious matter?

The document is cogent and concise. The authors understand how to argue the case, how to present questions, and how to expose the reality – even in very delicate situations. At the same time, the work is praiseworthy for the notable historical panorama it unfolds. It is encouraging to see that the traditionalist current counts among its members such an inestimable intellectual team as the four signers of *An Urgent Plea.*

The style is elevated and the language is clear. At the same time, the tone is firm and respectful in its address to the Pope. In short, it is a distinguished work with *élan.*

It is, therefore, with satisfaction that *Tradition in Action, Inc. (TIA)* offers to the public *An Urgent Plea: Do Not Change the Papacy* in book form, as it did one year ago with the statement *We Resist You to the Face.*

The text of the document is the responsibility of the four authors. *TIA* assumes sole responsibility for the pictures and captions.

Los Angeles, May 5, 2001
Patrick J. Odou
Secretary, *TIA, Inc.*

# TABLE OF CONTENTS

*Tradition In Action* dedicates this work
to St. Gregory VII (1073-1085),
the Pope *par excellence*.

The painting by Federico Zuccari presents the
symbolic episode of Canossa.
In January 1077, Emperor Henry IV humbly
kisses the foot of the Pontiff as he begs pardon
for his past crimes against the Papacy.

# AN URGENT PLEA:
# DO NOT CHANGE THE PAPACY

**An open letter to Pope John Paul II by lay Catholics regarding the announced reform of the Papacy**

by

Catholic Journalists

Atila Sinke Guimarães

Michael J. Matt

John Vennari

Marian Therese Horvat, Ph.D.

# AN URGENT PLEA:
# DO NOT CHANGE THE PAPACY

Your Holiness John Paul II,

After the many and controversial festivities for the passing of the Millennium, the beginning of the year 2001 ushered in strong winds of change in the Church. The year opened with numerous rumors and speculations about your eventual retirement, which would involve a reform of the Papacy and the choice of a new Pope.

These winds, however, were not new ones. Over the years, much had already been said about your retirement and the reform of the Papacy. The retirement would ostensibly be motivated by your weakening health. But is there not a certain inherent contradiction here? How could a person with such poor health follow an agenda of activities such as yours, which, few would deny, would normally prostrate a vigorous man of 50 years? Your numerous and wearying travels stand as testimony against these rumors. What other Head of State could manage, as you have, to make 20 or 30 speeches during the course of four or five days of travel, preside over innumerable ceremonies, receive countless persons without interruption, face enormous multitudes, and then return to Rome to take up again the burdensome day-to-day activities of an *aggiornato* Pope? The sacral Papacy of times past presupposed carefully selected public appearances, the issuance of solemn and infrequent documents, and the leading of a recollected life. The new style of Papacy of the post-Conciliar era has, in the minds

La Croix, Sept. 25, 1993

According to German Bishop Karl Lehmann,
recently named Cardinal, John Paul II
could have mental problems.

of many, transformed the Church into a stage and the Pope into a super-star. Obviously, this is more strenuous than the former style. However, since you are the one who chose this regime, if you so desired you could easily change it and arrange for a less exhausting schedule. One sees, therefore, that this argument of broken health is not overly convincing.

About one year ago, the German Bishop Karl Lehmann – recently elevated to Cardinal – had the indelicacy to raise publicly the possibility that your mental faculties had debilitated to the point that you should retire.[1] For anyone who even casually follows your many activities, it is clear that no lack of mental equilibrium can be noted in your very frequent written and spoken pronouncements or in the coherence of your line of government. In our opinion, it is progressivist – and we respectfully disagree with it[2] – but it is perfectly coherent, including its frequent strategic retreats. Therefore, the reasons that are being given for your retirement are not credible. Despite this, the hue and cry does not cease, but, to the contrary, increases.

One might say that some powerful and evil genie is demanding the reform of the Papacy and sounding a gong that calls for this to take place some time soon. The unfounded references to your weak physical and mental health seem merely a pretext to hasten this goal.

Since the beginning of the year, there have been more and more indications that the road is veering sharply

---

[1] *Los Angeles Times,* January 11, 2000, p. A1.
[2] See the open letter *We Resist You to the Face*, signed by the four authors of this *Plea* and published in *The Remnant* (April 30, 2000); *Tradition in Action* (book form – May 2000); *Catholic Family News* (July 2000).

toward a reform of the Papacy. From this perspective, therefore, Most Holy Father, we request your leave to trace the general lines that surround such a reform. We ask that Your Holiness correct us if we are wrong, and we would be honored with the courtesy of a response to our appeal, especially since it concerns an issue central to the lives of all Catholics.

The Cathedral of Notre Dame, where the National Council of the Constitutional Church met in 1797.

# Chapter I

## THE PLAN OF THE REFORM OF THE PAPACY: A REVOLUTIONARY, LIBERAL, AND MODERNIST DESIRE FOR MORE THAN 200 YEARS

Anyone who has followed the History of the Church even superficially over the last 200 years realizes that the desire to reform the Papacy is not a new plan. After the French Revolution and the establishment of the sadly celebrated *Civil Constitution of the Clergy*, the "French Constitutional Church" that surged was forged according to revolutionary philosophical principles and was opposed to the Papal Primacy. That attempt to curb the papal power ended as a futile experiment, condemned by the Church and put aside. Nonetheless, it represented a new formula that in certain aspects continued to live in the liberal Catholic movement; from there, those same ideas were subtly insinuated into the whole Church.

In the religious sphere, therefore, the French Revolution marked the installation of two important milestones: *First*, it established its Catholic counterpart of Liberalism, the father of Modernism and Progressivism.[3]

---

[3] Here we take Liberalism as the attempt to unify Catholic thinking with the ideas of the French Revolution in the political and social ambit. Modernism arises from an analogous attempt to reconcile Catholic thinking with German Idealism especially with the theory of Schleiermacher, which supposes a presence of an essential divine immanence in the human soul. Such a thesis was "translated" to Catholic language by Johann Adam Möhler and had a strong influence on German and French Modernism. This resulted in an immanentist

*Second*, it gave official status to the false notion that all religions are equal – a notion that was transformed into law on December 6, 1793. This gave birth to the religious indifferentism of the State, which also soon was condemned by the Pope. But an analogous error found its way inside the Church, namely the assertion of equality of religions, which *ipso facto* denies the unicity of the Catholic Church and the Papal Primacy. The documents of Vatican II *Dignitatis humanae* and *Unitatis redintegratio* represented respectively the embrace by the leaders of the Conciliar Church of the errors of religious indifferentism of the State and its acceptance in the spiritual sphere.

The humiliations to which Napoleon subjected Pius VI and Pius VII were, concretely and *manu militari* [by military force] attempts to subject the Popes to the Empire – the old Ghibelline dream in a French historical context. That is to say, it was yet another negation of the Papal Primacy.

---

Modernist thinking, primarily in the psychological ambit, and was justly denounced in the Encyclical *Pascendi Dominici gregis* by St. Pius X. Progressivism, which followed and took over Modernism, assumed the same principles as the latter. It also accommodated the thinking of the more recent German, French, and Danish Existentialism, which disregards abstract ideas in favor of what exists concretely. This provides the basis for the progressivist norm to emphasize the "pastoral" (practical) ecclesiastical activities, and to put aside the doctrinal orientation of the Catholic Church. Progressivism was characterized by a broader application of the aforementioned philosophical principles to the ecclesiastical life, namely the so-called biblical, patristic, and liturgical renewal. Also Progressivism presents a new conception of the Church – the Church as mystery and the Church as people of God. These currents of thought – Liberalism, Modernism, and Progressivism – are inter-changeable among themselves. They could be more precisely defined as three metamorphoses of the same process rather than three different movements.

*Right*, Pius VII (1800-1823), who refused Napoleon's demand to annex the Papal States to the Empire and to become his vassal.
*Pius VII*, David, Louvre

June 5, 1809. On Napoleon's orders, French soldiers carried off into captivity Pius VII, from his residence, the Quirinal Palace.
Engraving by Pirinelli

An engraving from the time of the French
Revolution shows the "people" destroying the
religious symbols (*left corner*), making a parody
of the Catholic Prelates by donning religious
vestments (*bottom right*), and carrying statues of
saints, standards and crucifixes to be smashed
in a public demonstration of hatred
against the Catholic Church.
The conciliar liturgical reform, initiated by
Paul VI, also either destroyed or put aside
most of the religious symbols.

Many leaders of the liberal movement soon appeared overtly inside the Church and began to call for changes and adaptations: Lammenais, Lacordaire, and Montalembert in France; Möhler, von Ketteler, and Döllinger in Germany; Gioberti and Rosmini in Italy; John Acton in England; O'Connell in Ireland; Sterckx, De Potter, and Dechamps in Belgium. Among the adaptations they wanted was the reform of the Papal Primacy.

There was also a healthy reaction against the attacks of Catholic Liberalism, represented among others by Joseph de Maistre with his *Du Pape* [On the Pope], Louis de Bonald with his *Théorie du pouvoir politique et religieux* [Theory of Political and Religious Power], Louis Veuillot with his *L'Illusion libérale* [The Liberal Illusion], Donoso Cortés with his *Ensayo sobre el Catolicismo, el liberalismo y el socialismo* [Essay on Catholicism, Liberalism, and Socialism], Jules Morel with his *Somme contre le Catholicisme liberal* [Summary against Liberal Catholicism], and Dom Prosper Guéranger with his *Éssai sur le naturalisme contemporain* [Essay on Present Day Naturalism]. This glorious counter-revolutionary movement of the 19th century extended through all of Europe. Designated as "papists" or "ultramontanes,"[4] such Catholics did not fear to confront Liberalism wherever it presented itself, but principally in the French arena – which was the decisive center for social-political issues, or on the Roman stage – the cradle for religious ideas.

---

[4] *Ultramontanism* and *ultramontane* [literally, beyond the mountain] were terms invented by French liberals to describe the doctrines and policies that upheld the full authority of the Holy See and the Pope. The term *ultramontane* was used down until the end of the 19th century, especially at the time of Vatican Council I, to describe both a supposed exaggeration of papal prerogatives and those who supported them.

"Leo XIII, highly respectable from numerous points of view, also is known for important concessions to the liberal movement."

Those undaunted Catholics deserve much of the credit for creating a climate propitious for the acceptance of the dogma of Papal Infallibility and the Petrine Primacy that was solemnly declared by Pius IX in union with Vatican Council I in the Constitution on the Church, *Pastor Aeternus* (July 18, 1870).

The pontificates of Gregory XVI and Pius IX represented a sound reaction to the errors of Liberalism and the affirmation of the papal prerogatives on the dogmatic level. That is, anyone who would not accept them would cease to be Catholic.

The long pontificate of Leo XIII was marked by a contradictory orientation. On the one hand, he continued the forceful conduct of his predecessors against certain enemies of the Church, and thus reaffirmed and stabilized the Papal Primacy. On the other hand, he was the one who installed the well-known politics of *ralliement* [reuniting], that is, the union of the Church with the French democratic regime born from the Revolution of 1789. By establishing that the Church could approve the principles of the new revolutionary democracy with few restrictions, he consciously or unconsciously planted its seeds in the Church. Thus the installing of democracy in the Church, regardless of the name one gives it – collegiality, conciliarity, synodality, communion, co-responsibility, etc. – can be attributed in part to the *ralliement* of Leo XIII. This policy, which began with the symbolic "toast of Algiers"[5] and the Encyclical *Au milieu des sollicitudes*

---

[5] In November of 1890, Cardinal Lavigerie, Archbishop of Algiers, took advantage of the occasion when the French Mediterranean war fleet was anchored in the city port to offer a banquet to the French Admiral and officers. The officers' corps of the French Navy was well known for its Catholic convictions and monarchist views. The Cardinal received his guests to the republican music of "La Marseillaise" – which was still not recognized as the national anthem.

St. Pius X: Modernism is "the synthesis of all heresies."

[Among the concerns], represented one of the first steps along an extensive road of adaptations. This route led the Church to the *aggiornamento* of John XXIII and to the Constitution *Gaudium et spes* of Vatican II, which represented the Council's official adaptation to the errors of the modern world. Thus, Leo XIII, highly respectable from numerous points of views, also is known for important concessions to the liberal movement.

St. Pius X entered into fierce combat against the errors of Liberalism, which had multiplied and grown under Leo XIII and metamorphosed into Modernism. St. Pius X strove to do all that he could to exterminate this evil, well defined as "the synthesis of all the heresies." But its roots ran very deep, and it continued to spread covertly in stealth and silence. Still, despite its remarkable expansion and conquest of important and eminent positions in the Catholic Church, many laymen persevere in believing, as we do, that it is the duty of all Catholics to continue to follow St. Pius X's advance to combat this insidious heresy.[6]

---

During dessert, the Cardinal raised a toast in favor of acceptance of the French Republic. In his prepared speech, he invited the officers to adhere to the recent policy of *ralliement* of Leo XIII and to the revolutionary democratic regime. The Admiral and the officers did not join the Cardinal in his homage. See Plinio Corrêa de Oliveira, *Nobility and Analogous Traditional Elites in the Allocutions of Pius XII* (Hamilton Press: 1993), Note 36, pp. 416-17.

[6] "In the circumstances, and although I myself, as a layman, have never been asked to take the oath against Modernism, I cannot but believe what Pope St. Pius X said about Modernism, that it constitutes 'the synthesis of all heresies,' and therefore I have the duty, a duty basically as binding upon me a Catholic as it is binding upon all Bishops, Priests, and Religious, to repudiate it, to reject it, to disavow it, and to fight with all our strength this hydra-headed heresy wherever it rears its ugly head – even in Rome itself or in any of its modern-day bureaus and departments. And if this be treason, or what some high

Sometime in the 1930s, Progressivism came to light. This was but an artful name to designate a type of Modernism that was, on the one hand, a more prudent, subtler, and more sophistic movement that dodged those strong condemnations of Modernism. On the other hand, it was more complete and encompassing in some aspects because it set forth a more extensive vision of man, the universe, and the Church.

It was during the pontificate of St. Pius X that a lay intellectual and politician, Antonio Fogazzaro, described the road to reform the Church and Papacy in his novel *Il Santo*. Speaking about the Modernist groups who continued their work despite the condemnations, Fogazzaro affirmed: "We are a good number of Catholics both inside and outside of Italy, ecclesiastics and laymen, who desire a reform in the Church. We want a reform without rebellion, carried out by the legitimate authority. We want reforms in religious instruction, reforms in the liturgy …. and reforms also in the supreme government of the Church. In order to achieve that, we need to create a public opinion that will induce the authorities to act according to our opinions, even if this takes 20, 30, or 50 years."[7]

The longings of Fogazzaro were effectively realized some 50 years later. He published these words in 1907. In 1958 the election of John XXIII was the landmark for the reform of the Church and the Papacy. Vatican II, which was announced on January 25, 1959, would take this reform much further.

---

placed princely gentlemen say is treason, let them make the most of it! In the end, the truth will prevail!" Walter Matt, Editorial, *The Remnant,* August 22, 1975, p. 15.

[7] Antonio Fogazzaro, *Il santo* (Milan, 1907), p. 38.

Paul VI, reading the opening speech of the second
session of Vatican Council II, in which he introduced
the subject of collegiality in the Papal powers.

*The Popes.* Eric John

Cardinal Giovanni Battista Montini, before he was elected Pope. The photo expresses well his strong determination. He was largely responsible for the reforms of Vatican II.

The Modernist dream of changing the ecclesiastical institution and eventually obtaining a Pope favorable to a revolution in the Mystical Body of Christ accords with the previously announced aims of Freemasonry in relation to the Church. This was demonstrated by the well-known anti-Modernist and anti-Masonic author Msgr. Henri Delassus, who transcribed documents from the highest Masonic authorities in Italy. One of these documents is *The Permanent Instruction of the Alta Vendita*,[8] addressed to other Masons. It reads: "Now then, in order to ensure a Pope with the necessary scope, we must first prepare a generation worthy of the kingdom we are dreaming of .... You have to see that your reputation is established .... you have to win the confidence of professors and students; you have to take special care that those who enter the ranks of the clergy are pleased with your meetings .... This reputation will allow your doctrine access to the young clergy and monasteries. In a few years, this clergy naturally will have invaded all the offices: they will govern, administer, judge, form the King's council, and choose the Pontiff who will reign. And this Pontiff, like most of his contemporaries, will be more or less imbued with the Italian and humanitarian principles that we will begin to put into circulation .... Let the clergy move forward under the banner of the Apostolic Keys. Cast your net like Simon-bar-Jonas; spread it to the depths of the sacristies, seminaries, and convents .... Even if at first your nets are empty, we promise you a catch even more miraculous than his .... You will have fished a revolution dressed in the [Pope's] tiara and cape, carrying the cross

---

[8] The Italian expression *alta vendita* means high lodge. This secret institution was the supreme Italian Masonic authority when the cited document was released. It was the equivalent of the English Grand Lodge.

and [papal] flag, a revolution that will need only a small stimulus to set fire to the four corners of the earth."[9]

If we compare these grave words of the enemies of the Church to the present day progressivist plans, it leaves us very pensive...

\* \* \*

---

[9] "Instruction secrète permanente donnée aux membres de la Haute-Vente," in Henri Delassus, *La conjuration antichrétienne* (Lille: Desclée De Brouwer, 1910), vol. 3, pp. 1045-1047. On the consequences of this document in the Catholic milieu and its applications in the post-Conciliar period, see John Vennari, *The Permanent Instruction of the Alta Vendita* (Rockford: TAN, 1999), pp. 6-10.

# Chapter II

## Vatican II opened the doors for a reform of the Papacy

What is collegiality? The term refers to the College of Apostles, and, by extension, to the College of Bishops, successors of the former. Our Lord conferred certain powers to the Apostles *in genere* [in general], while He conferred others to Peter *in specie* [in particular]. The term collegiality, while completely legitimate in its etymology, is habitually utilized erroneously in the language of the Conciliar Church to signify that Jesus Christ would have given the same powers to all the Apostles, including Peter. Therefore, Peter should not have the primacy, the full and supreme authority over the other Apostles. In other words, the notion of the Petrine Primacy that the Church teaches would be wrong. What would be necessary is to reform the Papacy and to do away with the notion that the Sovereign Pontiff has supreme powers. The monarchical Papacy should be replaced with a new form of government in which all the Bishops would participate in the supreme power of the Church.

In the opening speech of the second session of Vatican Council II, Paul VI introduced the concept of collegiality in the powers of the Pope. He affirmed: "The Council should deepen our understanding of the doctrine of the Episcopate, its functions, and its relations with Peter. Thus the means that we will use to exercise our apostolic function in the doctrinal and pastoral plane will be explained. This universal function, which Christ bestowed with the plenitude and legitimate efficacy of power that you know, could nonetheless receive a greater

The Bishops climb.
The powers of the Episcopacy have been rising steadily –
to the detriment of the Papal Primacy.

support and assistance if our brothers in the Episcopate .... would render us, by means and methods that it will be necessary to establish opportunely, an assistance that is more active, more considerable, and more conscious of the mission you have received."[10]

In the second session on October 30, 1963, the directors of the Council submitted to a vote four questions about the College of Bishops. The third one was this: Does the Body or College of Bishops, as successor of the College of Apostles and always in communion with the Pope who is its head, possess the supreme power of the Universal Church? To this question, 1,808 Bishops responded "yes" and only 336 said "no." The fourth question was: Does this power belong to the College by divine right? Here, 1,717 Bishops responded "yes," and only 408 said "no."[11] These two votes meant that already at the second session of the Council many Bishops gave their adhesion to an erroneous notion of the supreme power of the Church. These unexpected ruptures with the perennial Catholic Magisterium were among the most expressive victories of Progressivism in Vatican II.

With such an "electoral" basis, the concept of collegiality was introduced in the Constitution *Lumen gentium*. In the official text, one can read: "Together with its head, the Roman Pontiff, and never without this head, the episcopal order is the subject of supreme and full power over the universal Church .... The supreme authority with which this College is empowered over the

---

[10] Paul VI, *Solenne inizio della seconda sessione del Concilio Ecumenico Vaticano II*, *Insegnamenti di Paolo VI* (Vatican: Tipografia Poliglotta, 1965), pp. 174-175; René Laurentin, *Bilan de la deuxième session* (Paris: Seuil, 1964), pp. 30-31.
[11] R. Laurentin, ibid., p. 104.

The Synods, established by Paul VI,
are being prepared to receive deliberative,
and not just consultative, powers. This could
transform the Synod into a *de facto* powerful Upper
House. The Pope would no longer be a sovereign,
but a type of president or constitutional monarch.
*Above*, Prelates leave an assembly of
the 1988 Synod (Rome).

whole Church is exercised in a solemn way through an Ecumenical Council" (n. 22b).[12]

Although in other parts of the same paragraph it recognizes an accidental primacy of papal power, the position of *Lumen gentium* essentially places papal power on equal footing with the power of the College or the Council.[13] It establishes that the fullness of the Church's power normally would be exercised when both the Pope and the College speak jointly. This supposed dependence of the fullness of papal power on the College or Council is an attempt to destabilize the power of the Church. It rests on the assumption that the Pope/College or Pope/Council relationship would receive greater assistance from the Holy Ghost and be more representative of Christ than when the Pontiff acts by himself.

This sophism is based on a semantic misunderstanding about what the fullness of Church power actually is and who exercises it. From this comes a consequent juridical and theological confusion.

---

[12] The doctrine on collegiality in *Lumen gentium* provoked much discussion, during which requests were made for the introduction of a *Preliminary Explanatory Note*. This note, added in order to satisfy some conservative Bishops, is in blatant contradiction with what is affirmed in the text as well as the general interpretation given to collegiality after the Council. On the topic of this *Explanatory Note,* see A. S. Guimarães, *In the Murky Waters of Vatican II* (Metairie, La.: Maeta, 1997), Chap VI, §§ 61-62, 101-102.

[13] On this topic the intention of the authors of the present *Plea* is not to open an academic discussion on possible interpretations of *Lumen gentium* according to tradition. Such a discussion would be endless, because the official text itself pays tribute to ambiguity. We place ourselves in a practical perspective: since Vatican II, the doctrine of collegiality in *Lumen gentium* has been constantly applied to increase the powers of the Bishops in accordance with what we state in the text.

Pope Leo III crowns Charlemagne Emperor of the
Holy Roman Empire. It was the recognition of the
supremacy of the Pope over not only all the Church,
but also over the temporal sphere.
*The Coronation of Charlemagne* by Raphael, Vatican

The truth is that in the Church, the full visible power is the supreme power of the Pope to teach and govern, derived, by divine mandate, from the power of Our Lord Jesus Christ and the continuous assistance of the Holy Ghost. This supreme power of the Pope is exercised in the use of his broadest prerogatives as Vicar of Christ.

There is an undeniable accidental fullness of the power to teach when a doctrinal definition is made by the Pontiff together with a Council or the ensemble of the Bishops dispersed throughout the world. This accidental fullness derives from the desire of the Pope himself to confer to his decision a certain solemnity, which signifies that he is making use of all his power. The unanimous or partial agreement of the College, or even its hypothetical rejection of a solemn act of teaching or governing of the Pontiff, would not alter the essence of the decision. The Pope's full power lies in his supreme prerogative as Vicar of Christ. The submission or rejection of the College or Council to the Pope's decision would be a different question outside the terrain of the origin and plenitude of this power. This would be a moral and disciplinary question, which is not the case to deal with here.

To suppose that an essential fullness of the power of the Church to teach and govern would be exercised by both the Bishops and the Pope would change the very nature of this power. It would imply that its source is not divine and that such power was not delegated by Christ to one man alone: "Thou art Peter, and upon this rock I shall build my Church" (Mt 16:18). It would promote the notion that this power resides in the College of Bishops. With regard to the power to govern, this would deny the Papal Monarchy and would transform the Holy Catholic Church into a Church in which the Holy Pontiff would be reduced in essence to the role of either a president or a constitutional monarch, obedient to the norms that issue from the College. This is unacceptable and condemned by Catholic teaching.[14] However, even though this has been condemned, it seems that this is, in fact, what is now a desired objective in the proposed reform of the Papacy.

"And upon this rock I shall build my Church."

---

[14] See some condemnations below, Chap.6B.

# Chapter III

## SINCE THE COUNCIL, WELL KNOWN PRELATES AND THEOLOGIANS HAVE ASKED FOR THE REFORM OF THE PAPACY

Several of the principal players who inspired the documents of Vatican II and oriented their application and whose progressivist theses are today considered as reference points in ecclesiastical thinking, have advocated a radical change in the power of the Papacy. We will cite a few examples.

Cardinal Yves Congar clearly opposes the dogma defined by Pius IX and the First Vatican Council when he affirms: "Some say that only the Pope has universal jurisdiction [government] in the Church, and that the jurisdiction of the Bishops proceeds from him. In my opinion, this thesis is absolutely unacceptable …. In the opposite sense, a second thesis holds that the power of the Church, even the power of the Pope, would always act as 'head of the College.' He could not act by his own power as Vicar of Christ …. I strongly favor a collegial power that can be exercised by the College of the Bishops as well as by the Pope himself as its head, representing the whole body."[15]

The same author delineates the future he desires for the Church: "The ecclesiology of the people of God will deepen into an ecclesiology of communion and fraternity. What took place at the extraordinary Synod of 1969 is quite significant and interesting. After considering the

---

[15] *Jean Puyo interroge le Père Congar* (Paris: Centurion, 1975), pp. 209-210.

*30 Dias*. March 1993

*Above*, Fr. Yves Congar, O.P. (*center*) at work during the Council. The French Dominican actively collaborated in 10 of the 16 final documents. Afterward, he was made a Cardinal by John Paul II as a reward for his labor.

*30 Giorni*. June 1985

Three of the four Cardinals chosen by Paul VI to direct the sessions of Vatican II. The three were well known for their progressivist orientation. *From left*, the Belgian Leo Josef Suenens, the German Julius Döpfner, and the Italian Giacomo Lercaro.

College and the collegial act in its strict juridical sense, they went on to the consideration of 'collegiality' .... This means that the juridical domain and that of cooperation and co-responsibility have come together in the notion of communion .... Precisely because one shares the same goods, that is, the same mission (*cum munus*), one is in communion .... This also continued the movement that allowed Vatican II to overcome the tendency that has characterized the history of ecclesiology, at least in the West, which is to isolate structures of authority and to develop them separately. Instead, they began to find themselves inserted into the communities as a functional service."[16]

The thinking of the progressivist Jesuit, Fr. Karl Rahner, S.J., considered by many as one of the greatest theologians of the 20th century, exerted a remarkable influence in the documents of Vatican II. On the topic of papal power, he states: "The Bishops are subordinate executives of the Holy Father in what refers to daily affairs; in this they submit to the central authority of Rome. The Bishops consider the Nuncio of His Holiness as his representative and their immediate superior. This concept, however, is opposed to Catholic doctrine .... The supreme power of the Church is exercised through the mediation of the Bishops; this was declared and reiterated with all solemnity in Vatican Council II."[17]

Cardinal Julius Döpfner, one of the four moderators directing the sessions of Vatican II, clearly adopted the erroneous position we pointed out in Chapter II. He definitively linked the papal power to the College of

---

[16] Yves Congar, "Strutture essenziali per la Chiesa di domani," in V.A. *L'avvenire della Chiesa* (Brescia: Queriniana, 1970), pp. 211-214.
[17] K. Rahner, "El principio sinodal," in *La reforma que llega de Roma* (Barcelona: Plaza & Janes, 1970), pp. 21-22.

Fr. Karl Rahner, S.J.
(*below*), one of the
principal thinkers of the
progressivist current.
Some of his theses were
introduced in the most
important documents of
Vatican II.

*30 Dias*, July 1990

*Above*, Fr.
Rahner with his
disciple, Fr. Josef
Ratzinger,
working together
at the Council.

*30 Dias*, Jan. 1991

Bishops as a whole: "Vatican Council II is important for its concept of the Papacy, above all because of the relationship it makes between papal power and College of Bishops. Until now, the Pope related principally with Bishops individually; now the Pope and the College of Bishops are placed side by side in a more accentuated way. Hence it appears evident that the College of Bishops holds the supreme power of the Church in the same way; that is, it has the power to teach infallibly and to guide the people of God on the path of salvation, which relates and will always relate to the Pope alone. Nonetheless, it is certain that the College of Bishops and the Pope do not hold such power independently, but only when intimately linked together."[18]

Cardinal Suenens, another of the four moderators of the Council, takes an ecumenical approach in his defense of a new formulation for the exercise of the Papacy: "For ecumenical as well as theological reasons, it is necessary to avoid any formulations of the mission of the Pope that isolate him from the College of Bishops, of which he is the head. When it is emphasized that the Pope has the right to act and to speak 'alone,' the word 'alone' never means 'separately' or 'in isolation.' Even when the Pope acts without the formal collaboration of the Episcopal Body – as he has the legal right to do – he always acts as its head."[19] In fact, Suenens practiced what he preached. He was the one who, in 1968, spearheaded the worldwide revolt against *Humanae vitae*, on the

---

[18] J. Döpfner, *La Chiesa viventi oggi* (Bari: Paoline, 1972), pp. 220-221.

[19] L.J. Suenens, *Souvenirs et esperances* (Paris: Fayard, 1991), p. 173.

grounds that Pope Paul VI had issued the Encyclical in an alleged "non-collegial" manner.[20]

The revolutionary Fr. Hans Küng defends analogous principles: "A reunification of the separated Christian churches is absolutely inconceivable and unfeasible if viewed in the light of the present Roman system, which continues to be centralist .... But the situation would change completely if the Bishop of Rome were to clearly delimit his sphere of competence in relation to the various services."[21]

Küng also advises some practical measures to be instituted: "The authoritarian system of a one-man regime finds support neither in the original constitution of the Church based on the New Testament, nor in today's democratic mentality. Hence it must be replaced by a collegial government of the Church at all levels .... Representative groups should be guaranteed not only the right of consultation, but also of decision-making."[22]

He also demands: "As for the election of the Pope, it has become particularly urgent that the College of Cardinals, which is absolutely unrepresentative and

---

[20] In *Humanae vitae*, Paul VI reinforced the traditional condemnation of birth control despite the fact that the Vatican's 68-member birth-control commission had voted overwhelmingly to change the Church's teaching against contraception. Following Cardinal Suenens' lead, liberal theologians, such as those guided by Fr. Charles Curran, and the Canadian Bishops at Winnipeg, dissented from *Humanae vitae* based on the so-called "non-collegial nature" of its promulgation. It was Cardinal Suenens who provided the rationale for their revolt. For details see "The Charismatic Cardinal Suenens," John Vennari, (Parts I, II), *Catholic Family News*, October and December 1997.

[21] Hans Küng, *A Igreja* (Lisbon: Moraes, 1969), vol. 2, pp. 317-318.

[22] H. Küng, *Veracidade – O futuro da Igreja* (São Paulo: Herder, 1969), pp. 178-179.

completely anachronistic, hand over the election to a Council of Bishops and lay people."[23]

These are only a few examples of some of the more expressive Prelates and theologians from the progressivist current who want the Papacy to be changed.

*Left,* Fr. Hans Kung, whose polemical works attack Papal Infallibility and assert there are no longer differences between the Holy Church and Protestantism.
*30 Dias,* Jan. 1991

Secretary of State, Cardinal Angelo Sodano (*right*), recently praised one of the works of Hans Küng titled *Christianity, Essence and History,* thus lending prestige to the revolutionary German theologian.
*Golias,* Sept./Oct. 1996

---

[23] Ibid., p. 179.

*Right*, John Paul II signing
the Encyclical *Ut unum sint*
on May 25, 1995.
*Below*, The magazine
*Inside the Vatican*
headlined John Paul II's
revolutionary "offer to
change the way papal
primacy functions."

*Corriere della Sera May 31, 1995*

INSIDE THE VATICAN

JUNE-JULY 1995 $5/£3.50/1800

FOR THE SAKE OF UNITY
In a dramatic gesture,
aimed at ending centuries
of Christian division,
John Paul II offers
to change the way
papal primacy functions

CAN
THE
PAPACY
CHANGE?

# Chapter IV

## THIS DESIRE FOR REFORM WAS TAKEN UP BY YOUR HOLINESS IN THE ENCYCLICAL *UT UNUM SINT*

Contrary to what would have been expected, Your Holiness took up this progressivist agenda for the reform of the Papacy. Alleging that "the path of ecumenism is irrevocable,"[24] and that it constitutes "a duty of the Christian conscience"[25] – statements disputable in themselves – you proposed changing the traditional doctrine of the Papal Primacy in order to remove the "difficulty" that the Papacy causes for Protestants and Schismatics. In your Encyclical *Ut unum sint,* you gave new emphasis to words you had already spoken: "As I acknowledged on the important occasion of a visit to the World Council of Churches in Geneva on June 12, 1984, the Catholic Church's conviction that in the ministry of the Bishop of Rome she has preserved .... the visible sign and guarantor of unity constitutes a difficulty for most other Christians" (n. 88).

To remove this "difficulty," you assume the responsibility of this reform: "I am convinced that I have a particular responsibility in this regard, above all in acknowledging the ecumenical aspirations of the majority

---

[24] "At the Second Vatican Council, the Catholic Church committed herself irrevocably to following the path of the ecumenical venture" (*Ut unum sint*, n. 3a).
[25] "The Catholic Church embraces with hope the commitment to ecumenism as a duty of the Christian conscience" (Ibid., n. 8c, 15a).

*La Contre Réforme Catholique. Aug. 1994.*

December 7, 1991 - An ecumenical prayer at the Altar of the Confession in St. Peter's Basilica. A new Papacy emerges, no longer Catholic, but doctrinally elastic enough to encompass Schismatics and Protestants.

Ibid.

John Paul II praying at the World Council of Churches (Geneva). To be recognized by Schismatics and Protestants, the new Papacy would become only a "presidency of love." In fact, neither the Protestants nor Schismatics accept the dogmas of Papal Infallibility and the Petrine Primacy.

of the Christian communities and in heeding the request made of me to find a way of exercising the Primacy which, while in no way renouncing what is essential to its mission, is nonetheless open to a new situation" (n. 95b).

You have expressed the desire that, together with the Protestants and Schismatics, a search for a new way of exercising the Primacy should be made. In fact, you affirmed: "I insistently pray the Holy Spirit to shine his light upon us, enlightening all the pastors and theologians of our churches, that we may seek, together of course, the forms in which this ministry may accomplish a service of love recognized by all concerned" (n. 95c).

Further on, you even insisted upon receiving the doctrinal collaboration of heretics and Schismatics in order to model the new face of the Papacy: "This is an immense task, which I cannot refuse and which I cannot carry out by myself. Could not the real but imperfect communion existing between us persuade church leaders and their theologians to engage with me in a patient and fraternal dialogue on this subject, a dialogue in which, leaving useless controversies behind, we could listen to one another, keeping before us only the will of Christ?" (n. 96).

Thus, there is not the least doubt that you are the principal impelling force for the reform of the Petrine Primacy.

However, an important question still remains to be answered. How would you construct the "reformed" face of the Papacy? What you have written in *Ut unum sint* offers some indication.

Basing yourself on the Decree *Unitatis redintegratio* of Vatican II, you are committed to make "every effort to eliminate words, judgments, and actions which do not respond to the condition of separated

*Inside the Vatican.* Jan. 2001

In a symbolic gesture that signifies his desires for the future, John Paul II invited a Schismatic and a Protestant to the ceremony of the opening of the Holy Doors for the Third Millenium at St. Paul's Outside the Walls.

brethren with truth and fairness and so make mutual relations between them more difficult" (*UR* n. 4b; *UUS* n. 29). How can this norm be applied to the Papacy, since the Protestants deny even the need for its existence and the Schismatics are in a millennium-old revolt against it? It seems that we are walking toward an effective negation of the makeup of the Papacy by which only some of its appearances would be maintained.

Another principle that you adopted for this proposed reform is that "the manner and order in which Catholic belief is expressed should in no way become an obstacle to dialogue with our brethren" (*UR* n. 11a; *UUS* n. 36c). Thus, should one "in no way" make a re-affirmation of the dogmas of Papal Infallibility and the Petrine Primacy, because both are clear obstacles to the desired pan-religious unity?

According to your words, the *first characteristic* of the new Papacy is collegiality: "When the Catholic Church affirms that the office of the Bishop of Rome corresponds to the will of Christ, she does not separate this office from the mission entrusted to the whole body of Bishops, who are also 'vicars and ambassadors of Christ.' The Bishop of Rome is a member of the 'College,' and the Bishops are his brothers in the ministry" (*UUS* n. 95a). Everything seems to indicate that we are facing the same error taught in *Lumen gentium* (n. 22b), pointed out above. That is to say, the supreme power of the Church would not be the power of the Roman Pontiff, but that of the College, of which the Pope is but a part.

The *second characteristic* that you present for the revolution in the Papacy involves the keynote of power. Instead of maintaining the power to command that it has had up until now, the papal "power" would come to be simply the capacity to serve: "The authority proper to this [papal] ministry is completely at the service of God's

At the World Day of Prayer for Peace (Assisi, October 27, 1986), a figure in white stands out at the microphone among an ensemble of representatives of the world religions. There is not even a raised step or platform to distinguish him from the others. This is symbolic of the progressivist longings for the new role of the Papacy. No more distinction. No more hierarchy. Just a horizontal reference point to hold together the whole.

merciful plan, and it must always be seen in this perspective. Its power is explained from this perspective" (*UUS* n. 92b).

How does Your Holiness understand this "service of God's merciful plan"? You identify it with ecumenism: "Ecumenism is not only an internal question of the Christian communities. It is a matter of the love which God has in Jesus Christ for all humanity" (n. 99). Further on you argue that the Three Persons of the Holy Trinity would be working for the success of ecumenism: "There is no doubt that the Holy Spirit is active in this [ecumenical] endeavor and that he is leading the church to the full realization of the Father's plan, in conformity with the will of Christ" (n. 100). In a text already quoted, you speak straightforwardly: "This ministry may accomplish a service of love recognized by all concerned [the pastors and theologians of our Christian churches]" (n. 95c). Thus, the Papacy you desire would be a "service" to achieve the union of religions without asking the non-Catholic confessions to make a conversion from their false creeds. At times this pan-religious aim is ambiguously presented under the goal of "the unity of the Church."[26] It is not necessary to point out that until Vatican II such an ecumenism was constantly condemned by the Catholic Magisterium.

---

[26] On December 5, 1996 the *Vatican Information Service* posted on the Holy See's Internet site a summary of the official press release of a three-day symposium on the Papal Primacy. Schismatic and Protestant theologians actively participated in this symposium promoted by the Congregation for the Doctrine of the Faith. The official summary states: "The collegial nature of the Episcopate, in fact, includes the function of the Primacy. In this context the Petrine ministry appears as if it were at the service of Church unity, intimately bound to the mission of evangelization."

The *third characteristic* presented in your Encyclical is the installation of a new type of primacy for the Papacy, a presidency of love: "Do not many of those involved in ecumenism today feel a need for such a [Petrine] ministry? A ministry which presides in truth and love so that the ship – that beautiful symbol which the World Council of Churches has chosen as its emblem – will not be buffeted by the storms and will one day reach its haven" (n. 97b).

These are the general features of the new face of the Papacy that you have outlined in the Encyclical *Ut unum sint*.

*    *    *

# Chapter V

## THIS PLANNED REFORM OF THE PAPACY
## IS BEING PRAISED
## BY VARIOUS PROGRESSIVIST THEOLOGIANS

Lately there has been a lot of discussion on the topic of this reform. Some of the American sources include the book *The Reform of the Papacy* by Archbishop John Quinn (1999); the book *Papal Primacy in the Third Millennium* by Russell Shaw (2000); a series of articles in the Jesuit magazine *America*: "The Millennium and the Papalization of Catholicism" (April 9, 2000) by John O'Malley, "The Papacy for a Global Church" (July 15, 2000) by Avery Dulles; "The Papacy for an Ecumenical Age: A Response to Avery Dulles" (October 21, 2000) by Ladislas Orsy; the article "Toward a New and Improved Primacy," by Ann Carey (*Our Sunday Visitor*, November 19, 2000); and the article "The Papacy under review" by Richard McBrien (*The Tidings*, Los Angeles, December 1, 2000). These numerous writings give the impression that there may have been some recent directive to address the subject so as to create a climate propitious for exactly such a reform. The news and articles about the subject reached an apex after the official convocation of an extraordinary Consistory to meet May 21-24, which would address the topic of the Petrine ministry and episcopal collegiality. Further, almost all of these works claim that their critiques and suggestions are in response to the requests of Your Holiness in the Encyclical *Ut unum sint.*

We ask your leave to present by way of example some excerpts from the book of Archbishop Quinn, *The*

Russell Shaw

"Lately there has been a lot of discussion on the topic of this reform. Some sources include *The Reform of the Papacy* by Archbishop John Quinn (1999) and *Papal Primacy in the Third Millennium* by Russell Shaw (2000).

Reviews of both books are available from *TIA, Inc.*

Archbishop John Quinn boldly accepted the Pope's invitation in *Ut unum sint* (1995) to modify the Petrine Primacy to accommodate the Schismatics and Protestants – an impossible task.

UT UNUM SINT: STUDIES ON PAPAL PRIMACY

THE
# REFORM
OF THE
# PAPACY

THE COSTLY CALL TO
CHRISTIAN UNITY

JOHN R. QUINN

*Reform of the Papacy* (Chapter I). In response to the requests of Your Holiness for suggestions to change the Papacy, Msgr. Quinn establishes this presupposition: Since the publication of your Encyclical, any reform or revolution in the Papacy relies entirely upon the "revolutionary" character of your document. He copiously cites *Ut unum sint* to prove this presupposition. In fact, Quinn argues: "The Encyclical of Pope John Paul II on Christian unity .... must also be called a revolution. For the first time, it is the Pope himself who raises and legitimizes the question of reform, and change in the papal office in the Church".[27]

Further on, he again cites your Encyclical to demonstrate his presupposition: "The search for unity [with the other religions] must pervade the whole life of the Church. This is another example of the revolutionary character of this Encyclical. Until the Second Vatican Council, ecumenism was regarded as dangerous to Faith, and only tried and true experts engaged in it very cautiously, if at all. Here the Pope is saying that it must pervade everything in the Church." [28]

Quinn offers still more evidence: "Another sign of the revolutionary character of this Encyclical are these words of the Pope: 'This is a specific duty of the Bishop of Rome .... I carry out this duty [the quest for unity among religions] with the profound conviction that I am obeying the Lord' (*UUS* n. 3-4)." [29]

---

[27] John R. Quinn, *The Reform of the Papacy – The Costly Call to Christian Unity* (New York: Herder & Herder, 1999), pp. 13-14.

[28] Ibid., p. 17.

[29] Ibid., p. 18. For convenience sake, we quote here paragraph 3c from the Encyclical *Ut Unum Sint*: "I myself intend to promote every suitable initiative aimed at making the witness of the Catholic community understood in its full purity and consistency, especially considering the engagement which awaits the Church at the threshold

"These numerous writings [on a change of the Papacy] give the impression that there may have been some recent directive to address the subject so as to create a climate propitious for such a reform."

The former Archbishop of San Francisco presents yet another argument: "Still another revolutionary feature of this Encyclical, the invitation to join the search for a new way of exercising the Primacy, is not confined only to Orthodox and Catholic Bishops and theologians. The Pope addresses all Christian churches and communions, issuing the same invitation: 'Could not the real but imperfect communion existing between us persuade Church leaders and their theologians to engage with me in a patient and fraternal dialogue on this subject ....?' (*UUS* n. 96)." [30]

With regard to the revolutionary character of the papal document, the author's conclusion seems indisputable: "The Encyclical *Ut unum sint* is clearly precedent breaking and, in many respects, revolutionary. It calls for a discussion of the Papacy by all Christians with the goal of finding a new way of making it more a service of love than of domination. It holds up the synodal [democratic] model of the Church in the first millennium and emphasizes that the Pope is a member of the College of Bishops and that the Primacy should be exercised in a collegial manner." [31]

Your Holiness certainly was not shocked by the affirmations of the American Prelate since, as soon as his book was published, he offered you a copy in a private audience with which Your Holiness honored him. According to Vatican conventions, you would have been informed beforehand of the contents of the work.

---

of the new Millenium. That will be an exceptional occasion, in view of which she asks the Lord to increase the unity of all Christians until they reach full communion. The present Encyclical letter is meant as a contribution to this most noble goal. Essentially pastoral in character, it seeks to encourage the efforts of all who work for the cause of unity."

[30] Ibid., p. 22.

[31] Ibid., p. 34.

Therefore, to all appearances, the audience that you granted to Archbishop John Quinn represented a tacit approval of his conclusions about the revolutionary character of your Encyclical.

Everything seems to indicate, therefore, that we are walking in the direction toward which Msgr. Quinn pointed – a revolution in the Papacy.

Archbishop John R. Quinn: "The Encyclical
*Ut unum sint* is clearly precedent breaking
and, in many respects, revolutionary."
*Actualité Religieuse*, Jan. 15, 1997

# Chapter VI

## COLLEGIALITY IN THE POWERS OF THE POPE

Based on the above disturbing facts, the possibility of a revolution in the Papacy is a most serious matter that demands urgent measures to avoid a great damage to Holy Mother Church. Consequently, we feel compelled to bring to the attention of Your Holiness, as Universal Doctor of the Church, the traditional doctrine of the Magisterium on the powers of the Petrine Primacy. We do this knowing full well your awareness of all that will now be presented. With deepest respect and humility we ask: how can such a revolution in the Papacy be possible in light of the clear, consistent, and traditional Magisterial doctrine regarding the Primacy of Peter?

## A – Catholic Doctrine on the powers of the Pope

The Pope has three powers: the power to sanctify, the power to teach and the power to govern. Each of these powers has special characteristics.

The power to sanctify, or the power of Orders, is the power to say the Holy Mass and to administer the Sacraments. It is, therefore, the power to confer the Sacrament of Holy Orders (to consecrate Bishops and ordain priests), and to administer the other six Sacraments – Confirmation, Confession, Holy Communion, Extreme Unction, Matrimony, and Baptism.

This power was conferred by Our Lord equally on all the Apostles and to their successors, the Bishops. For this reason, the Pope has essentially the same power to

Total equality: The goal hiding behind
the controversial collegiality.

sanctify as the other Bishops. The Bishop also has the power to teach his flock and the power to govern his Diocese, but in these two last powers, he relies on the papal supreme powers to teach and govern. Therefore, he must obey the Pope, not so much because of the Pope's power to sanctify, but in view of his powers to teach and to govern. In fact, by the papal power to govern, the Bishops are chosen and established in their Dioceses. Their obedience is required in order to maintain the needed unity in the teaching and discipline of the Church. There is no reason to apply collegiality to the power to sanctify, because as such the Pope and Bishops have essentially the same power.

The power to teach was also conferred upon the twelve Apostles. However, it was conferred upon Peter over and above the others. For this reason, when the Pope speaks *ex cathedra* as the Universal Pastor and Doctor of the Church, he is infallible. According to the doctrine of Papal Infallibility, the certainty of the teaching of the Bishops relies directly on the Pope's power to teach, whether the Bishops are spread all over the world or whether they are joined together in council. The Pope's power to teach is not an absolute power; it is limited by the dogmas of Faith and by the ordinary and universal teaching of the Church throughout the preceding centuries. Thus, if a Pope teaches something different from traditional dogma and the perennial Magisterium, he should not be obeyed. To these doctrines general assent cannot be given and strict obedience must be denied. The

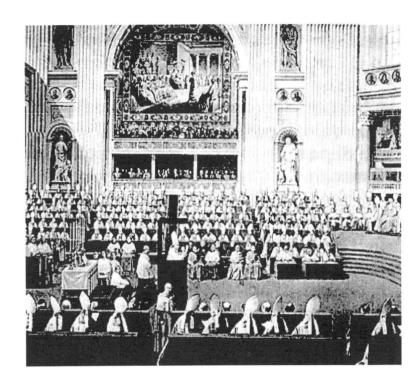

Pius IX with the First Vatican Council (*above*)
infallibly decreed: "If someone shall assert that the
Roman Pontiff possesses merely the principal part
and not all the fullness of the supreme power of
jurisdiction over the universal Church:
let him be anathema."

Bishops and even the faithful have the right and the duty to resist the erroneous teachings of that Pope.[32]

Certainly the Bishops have the power to teach because they, as heirs of the Apostles, received the divine mandate to preach the Gospel and they are Doctors of the Faith. But their teaching is not supreme, i.e., it must be judged by the Pope. If the Bishops' power to teach would have the same authority as that of the Pope, in a short time the unity of teaching and, after that, the unity of the Catholic Faith, would be broken. The Protestant and Schismatic sects are incapable of having unity in doctrine because they preach the equality of the power to teach. Those who want to apply collegiality to the power of papal teaching – that is, to consider the Bishops' power to teach as equal to that of the Pope – in reality want to transform the Catholic Church into something similar to these sects.

The Pope's power to govern, or the power of jurisdiction, is the most decisive. It includes the supreme

---

[32] "For example, we respectfully decline to believe that the death penalty must be outlawed and that criminals may never be put to death, as the Pope recently declared in *L'Osservatore Romano*. For example, we respectfully decline to believe that altar girls are a good thing for the Church, as the Pope declared in his *Letter to Women*. For example, we respectfully decline to believe that the New Mass is 'a great renewal' and that it is not inferior to the Old Mass, as the Pope declared in his address on the 25th anniversary of *Sacrosanctum Concilium*. For example, we respectfully decline to believe, as the Pope taught in *Ut unum sint,* that the ministers of Protestant sects which preach abortion are 'disciples of Christ' – a novel teaching His Holiness has confirmed again and again by conducting joint liturgical services with pro-abortion laymen pretending to be bishops. And, for example, we respectfully decline to believe that Islam is a religion deserving of divine protection, as the Pope taught when he declared 'May St. John Baptist *protect Islam* and all the people of Jordan . . .' at Wadi Al-Kharrar, on March 21, 2000." Michael J. Matt, Editorial, *The Remnant*, August 31, 2000.

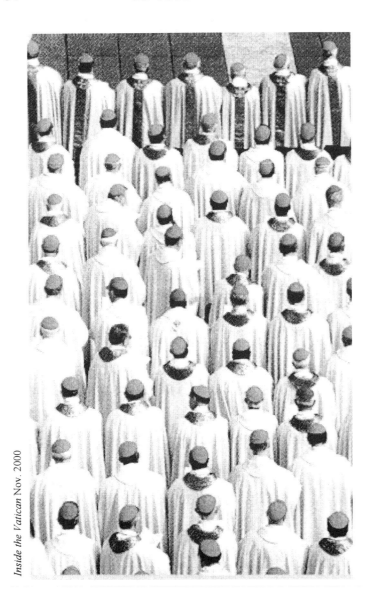

The progressivist doctrine of collegiality repeats the
condemned errors of past heresies.

power to act, legislate, judge, and punish. Traditionally, the Pope delegates most of the exercise of these powers to innumerable intermediary bodies of the Church – the Roman Congregations and the other Vatican Dicasteries: Tribunals, Pontifical Councils, Administrative Bodies, Special Committees, etc.[33] He also habitually delegates powers to Cardinals, Archbishops, Bishops, Nuncios, and Apostolic Delegates outside the Vatican. He reserves to himself the power to make final decisions or judge extraordinary cases. Thus while the Bishops have certain powers to govern, these are dependant on the supreme power of the Pope. Here again, we see that those who want to apply collegiality to the power of papal government – that is, to consider the Bishops' power to govern as equal to that of the Pope – in reality want to transform the Catholic Church into something similar to the Protestant and Schismatic sects.

The Church's regime of government emanates from an extremely rich reality. The Pope is elected by a vote of the College of Cardinals. The papal monarchy, therefore, issues from an aristocratic body, which democratically elects the successor to the Pontifical Throne. We have, therefore, the three regimes – monarchy, aristocracy, and democracy – proportionally represented in the Church. In the coronation ceremony, the Pope receives from Our Lord the "power of the Vicar" [*potestas vicaria*], that is, he comes to be the representative on earth *par excellence* of Jesus Christ, the one who acts in the place of Our Lord. This is the significance of the titles "Vicar of Christ" and "Sovereign Pontiff." Our Lord sanctions the new Pope during the ceremony of enthronement and

---

[33] Even here the delegation of powers made by the Sovereign Pontiff is limited. Thus it is wrong to say, as is sometimes alleged today, that if a Vatican Prelate performs (or claims to perform) any function in the name of the Pope – if a Prelate speaks, it is "the Pope speaking."

The new Papacy that is being planned can
represent the imprisonment of Peter.
*St Peter in Jail,* by Raphael, Vatican

bestows a divine stamp on the choice of the Cardinals. Therefore, over and above the human character of the election of a Pope, two divine characters are added – the representation of Christ and the special assistance of the Holy Ghost. In this specific sense, the governing regime in the Church is a monarchy of divine right, and its nature properly is defined as human-divine.

The human choice of the Pope, however, proceeds also from a vaster organic natural reality, which antedates the formation of the College of Cardinals. It is the reality of the Church herself, which was shaped through the centuries under the form of a feudal monarchy. Like every living reality, like a large family, the Church was gradually formed in function of her vitality and needs. Each Diocese has its own history, its special relations with the Holy See, its rights, and its privileges. For each country the Holy See has a special solicitude and provides assistance according to its apostolic needs. The Pope habitually respects the relative autonomy of the government of the Bishops, just as in a feudal monarchy the King respected the autonomy of his nobles. The Pope normally acts in accordance with the principle of subsidiarity – the superior power should act only when the inferior power shows itself incapable of fulfilling its mission. However, according to the Pope's discretion, he has the full right to intervene directly for any of the faithful of a Diocese independent of the concurrence of the Bishop, or even in opposition to him. Constantly orienting the individual Dioceses, the ecclesiastical Provinces and the countries' Episcopates that directed themselves to her, the Holy Church elaborated a system as perfect as possible to hear and be heard. This permits her to fulfill her mission faithfully and to make the exercise of government as just as possible.

*"One might say that some
powerful and evil genie is demanding
the reform of the Papacy..."*

*30 Dias*, Aug./Sept. 1991

This wise system of government caused the Catholic Church to become the human institution most cognizant of, and responsive to, every aspect of human reality. This is the opposite of a supposed exaggerated centralization that many theologians are criticizing today in order to advocate a reform. The system of government established in the Church is feudal – in the best sense of the word. That is, it is the wisely constituted government of the head over the body. This centralism has nothing of evil in itself. It is the normal centralism of the head in relation to the rest of the body that permits the head to direct all of the members well. To want to "reform" the present system in the Church in order to make the head equal to the body would be like trying to transform the Church with her divine-human likeness of the body and soul of Our Lord Jesus Christ into a resemblance of a jellyfish or other type of mollusk where the head and body are indistinguishable.

It seems to us, Holy Father, that any proposal of reform of the Papacy that does not clearly distinguish the three principal papal powers runs the serious risk of being confusing and detrimental. Often collegiality is requested on the basis of the fundamental equality of the Bishops in the power of Orders, but then it is followed by an attempt to apply it to the powers of teaching and of government. Without these clear distinctions of powers, many sophistic and false arguments for reforming the Papacy can appear convincing.

## B – Collegiality and the heresy of conciliarism in its full or mitigated form

We would like to present this item to Your Holiness as an inquiry. According to everything we have learned, we see that the power of government and the

"It is heretical to propose that the Roman Pontiff is ministerial head, if this is explained to mean that he received from the Church the power of his office." Pius VI, *Auctorem fidei*

According to the progressivist new look, the Pope would be only the head of the College of Bishops.

power of teaching of the Bishops come directly from the powers of the Pope in their full and supreme form, that is, from Papal Infallibility and the Petrine Primacy in the ecclesiastical Monarchy. At Vatican Council II and in the post-Conciliar period, arguments have been put forth that these powers have to become "participative" so as to end the monarchical character that distinguishes them. According to this view, the monarchical structure should be replaced by a regime that is "collegiate," that is to say, democratic. The power would not proceed from the one (the Pope) to the many (the Bishops); but it would be the opposite: the power would proceed from the many to the one. We see these initiatives as new versions of the errors of Conciliarism on an even broader scale, as we will explain below. Are we wrong? If this is the case, we ask the courtesy that you or some representative enter into a cordial dialogue with us to discuss the doctrinal points that may have escaped our analysis.

When the College of Bishops is understood as having the supreme power of government in the Church, obviously with the Pope included in the College, this is to affirm an even broader error than the claim that the Council has the supreme power of the Church. In effect, the Council is simply the College of Bishops solemnly convened together. When the College is not gathered together, it is dispersed throughout the world. Now, to affirm that the College has the supreme power, as Vatican

*30 Dias*, May 1990

According to one of the plans of the progressivist
agenda, after the resignation of John Paul II,
the next Conclave would elect more than one Pope to
divide the alleged "super-human" responsibility that
the Papacy would impose on a single man. Plans are
also underway to change the election of a Pope so that
the voters would no longer be only Cardinals, but
would include, among others, lay delegates and
representatives of the false religions.
*Above*, the last Conclave (1978) at the Sistine Chapel.

II did,[34] is the same as saying that the all of the Bishops – either dispersed or convened together – have the greatest power in the Church. We are, therefore, facing an even broader rendition of the errors of Conciliarism. This heresy affirmed that the Council had the supreme power in the Church, and if the Pope would not agree with the decisions of the Council, he should be deposed. This heresy of Conciliarism was erroneously sustained, among others, by the Council of Constance (1414-1418), the Council of Basel (1431-1437) and the Synod of Pistoia (1786).

Below are some papal documents that categorically condemn this conciliarist doctrine in either its full or mitigated form. It would seem that the collegiality that we are dealing with here would incur these same condemnations:

* In the Constitution *Pastor Aeternus*, Pius IX together with Vatican Council I excommunicated those who defend the following erroneous propositions: "If anyone should say that the Blessed Apostle Peter was not established by Our Lord as Prince of all Apostles and visible head of the Church Militant; or that he did not receive directly and immediately from the same Our Lord Jesus Christ the primacy of a true jurisdiction of his own, but only a primacy of honor: *let him be anathema*" (*DR* 1823).

* The same document stated: "If someone shall say that the Roman Pontiff has the office merely of inspection and direction, and not the full and supreme power of jurisdiction over the universal Church, not only in things which belong to Faith and Morals, but also in those which relate to the discipline and government of the Church spread through the world; or assert that he possesses

---

[34] *Lumen gentium* 22b; see text quoted above in Chapter II.

Farewell.
It is being said more and more frequently that John
Paul II will be the last Pope in History to hold the
plenitude of Papal Infallibility
and the Petrine Primacy.

merely the principal part and not all the fullness of this supreme power; or that this power which he enjoys is not ordinary and immediate, both over each and all the churches and over each and all the Pastors and the faithful: *let him be anathema*" (*DR* 1831).

* In the Constitution *Auctorem fidei* of August 28, 1794, Pius VI condemned the errors of the Synod of Pistoia: "Moreover, it is heretical to propose that *the Roman Pontiff is ministerial head*, if this is explained to mean that the Roman Pontiff received, not from Christ in the person of St. Peter, but from the Church, the power of his office by which, as the successor of Peter, the true Vicar of Christ, and the head of the entire Church, he has power over the universal Church" (*DR* 1503).

* In the Brief *Super soliditate* of November 28, 1786, Pius VI condemned the errors of Febronianism. The Brief is directed against Joseph Valentin Eybel, the Viennese canonist who wrote *Was ist der Papst?* [What is the Papacy?], based on the errors of the work by Febronius, *De statu Ecclesiae et legitima potestate Romani Pontifici* [On the State of the Church and the Legitimate Power of the Roman Pontiff], which was placed on the *Index* on February 27, 1764. Pius VI condemned the following errors:
     – "that every Bishop, as much as the Pope, was called by God to govern the Church and was granted the same power;
     – "that Christ granted the same authority to all the Apostles, and everything that one  believes can be obtained from and granted by the Pontiff alone, can also be obtained from any Bishop – either by virtue of his consecration or ecclesiastical jurisdiction;
     – "that Christ would have desired that the Church

be administered like a republic and, since this system of government requires a president for the sake of unity – that is, one who, without daring to meddle in the affairs of the other authorities, shares the powers of government – he conserves the privilege of exhorting the negligent to fulfill their duties. For the force of the Primate consists only in the prerogative of compensating for the negligence of others and assuring that unity is preserved by means of exhortation and example;

– "that the Pontiff has no power in other Dioceses, except in an extraordinary case;

– "that the Pontiff is the head which receives from the Church its strength and stability" (*DR* 1500).

Your Holiness, how can these strong and clear condemnations pronounced by prior Pontiffs harmonize with your desired reform of the Papacy? One could say that the points of your Encyclical that we quoted above directly incur these condemnations. Once again we ask: Are we wrong? Would it be possible to show us in what points? Why cannot a "patient and fraternal dialogue," similar to that which you solicited from Protestants and Schismatics on this theme, be opened with concerned and respectful Catholics like ourselves?

\*   \*   \*

# Chapter VII

## ECUMENISM AND THE REFORM OF THE PAPACY

The principal motive being given for the announced reform of the Papacy is the need to remove the great obstacle that it would represent for ecumenical unity. That is to say, if the present definition of the Papal Primacy were attenuated, then the Protestants and Schismatics would open their arms to unite with the Catholics.

Now, according to news reports in the national and international press, this supposition is false. The meager interest shown by the theologians of these false religions to your invitation to present their contributions to the reform of the Papacy stands as eloquent proof. Only a handful of publicly known proposals have arrived in response to your request,[35] and even then, one cannot exclude the

---

[35] In 1996 Robert MacFarlane wrote the article "An Anglican Response to the Encyclical *Ut unum sint," Ecumenical Trends* 25:12. In 1997 "Orthodox" theologian Olivier Clément published the book *Rome autrement.* The same year Waldensian scholar Paolo Ricca wrote the article "The Papacy in Discussion: Expectations and Perspectives," *One in Christ,* 33:283. In the same year, the Church of England published the observations *That They All May be One.* In 1998 Hermann J. Pottmeyer published the book *Towards a Papacy in Communion.* In May 1999 the ARCIC-II, the Second Anglican-Catholic International Commission issued *The Gift of Authority,* a document that intended to be a statement on the Papacy acceptable to Catholics and Anglicans. But far from that aim, it raised strong opposition in both religions, for example, from the progressivist Catholic theologian Hans Küng and the Anglican religious scholar Geoffrey Kirk.

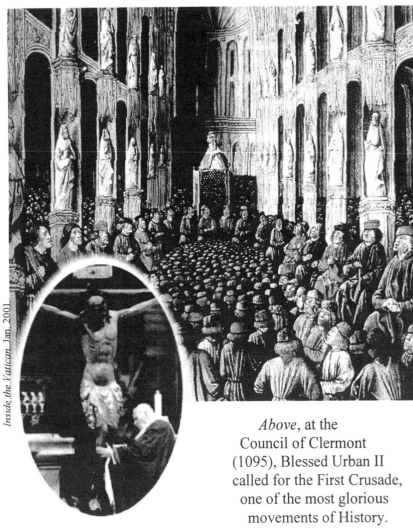

*Inside the Vatican,* Jan. 2001

*Above*, at the Council of Clermont (1095), Blessed Urban II called for the First Crusade, one of the most glorious movements of History.

*Above (inset),* John Paul II asked forgiveness for the Crusades at the Vatican (2000). This would be one of the conditions to make the Papacy acceptable to the Schismatics, Muslims, and Jews.

possibility that some of these suggestions were made at the instigation of the Vatican itself.

The proof of the collapse of ecumenism and inter-religious dialogue is not limited to only this. We could repeat here the documentation of the failure of ecumenism presented to Your Holiness in the book *Quo vadis, Petre?*.[36] It is a documentation all the more convincing in that it comes almost invariably from press sources that are promoting ecumenism. The book documents the failure of ecumenism and the inter-religious dialogue up to the year 1999. To update those facts, we ask leave to present, among many others, only few documents from authoritative sources that analyze the year 2000.

The topic of the failure of ecumenism is addressed in an interview by Mr. Andrea Riccardi, founder and president of the Community of Sant'Egidio,[37] a famous lay Catholic center that, along with other activities, promotes ecumenism. Its directors speak with a certain authority on the topic of ecumenism and orient many like-minded institutes for ecumenism.

In the interview, Riccardi tries to immunize his readers against those who "are pessimistic about the future of ecumenism." Attempting to bolster hope among its proponents, he offers these weak arguments: "We have not exhausted the dialogue among us [Christians]. Numerous problems persist, born from concrete situations.

---

[36] A. S. Guimarães, *Quo vadis, Petre?*, Chap. III, "Failures in the Internal Dynamics of Religious Politics" (Los Angeles: TIA, Inc., 1999), pp. 51-90.
[37] Andrea Riccardi, "Mon bilan du Jubilé," *Actualité des Religions*, Paris, January 2001, pp. 8-9.

CNN Internet Site. May 3. 2001

The Schismatic clergy strongly opposed John Paul II's
trip to Greece. Religious leaders yelled slogans that the
Pope was the "two-horned beast of the Apocalypse"
and "the Antichrist."
Carrying placards, they told him to "go home."
Certainly, a blatant failure of ecumenism.

For example, the problem of the Uniates,[38] the tensions between the Catholic Church and Russian Orthodox Church, and also between Moscow and Constantinople. On this level I fear a theological dialogue that could be transformed into technical diplomacy. In a contrary sense, I am convinced of the need for a 'dialogue of charity.' A dialogue that does not exclude the dimension of love."

The practical conclusion: Ecumenism is once again beached, left high and dry. The theological incompatibilities remain insoluble and threaten to spoil the "dimension of love."

Riccardi, as one who knows the subject well, explains the intentions of Your Holiness: "In *Tertio millennio adveniente,* John Paul II expressed a dream: 'We present ourselves on the occasion of the Grand Jubilee, if not totally united, at least much closer to overcoming the divisions of the Second Millennium.' He was hoping for a 'significant pan-Christian meeting' in Rome .... This meeting would have been a very important sign. He could not realize it in the year 2000. But in the near future it will be an obligatory step." Throughout the interview, the president of Sant'Egidio complains about the difficulties encountered by ecumenism. He ends by affirming, "pessimism is in fashion today."

This high-level confirmation of the failure of ecumenism also provides an indirect explanation of the reason why the planned pan-religious meeting did not take place in 1999 or 2000.

---

[38] Such "problems" would include, for example, the work of conversion carried out by the Ukrainian Catholics of the Eastern rite who are not obeying the ecumenical orientation of Rome as well as their attempts to reclaim the Catholic Churches that had been confiscated and given to the Schismatics under Communism. Marian T. Horvat, "Handing Over the Symbolic Icon of Our Lady of Kazan," *The Remnant,* January 31, 2001, p. 7.

Andrea Riccardi *(above, center),* founder and president of Sant'Egidio Community, one of the most influential lay societies that promote ecumenism and inter-religious dialogue.

*Left*, Geoffrey de Turckhein, a well-known French expert on ecumenism: "The euphoria over ecumenism is replaced with disillusion."

Referring to the inter-religious dialogue, Andrea Riccardi presents this bitter critique about the general orientation of the Vatican: "Was it absolutely necessary for the Jubilee to have assumed an inter-religious dimension? Frankly, I think that it was wrong to insist with the great religions that they participate in this principally Christian, or better, principally Catholic event. Numerous Protestants confessed that they were sympathetic neither to the idea of the Jubilee nor the way that it was conducted by the Vatican. Should we blame them for this? In Lisbon last October on the occasion of the inter-religious meeting promoted by Sant'Egidio, Jews and Muslims commented to me that these celebrations were a great manifestation of civilization. But it was something that did not touch internally on their respective traditions. We should resist the temptation to place ourselves, we Catholics, in the center of the world."

This clear affirmation of the collapse of the ecumenical and inter-religious initiatives of the Millennium comes from a source indisputably favorable to a pan-religion.

A French expert on ecumenism, Geoffroy de Turckheim, makes this synopsis of the situation at the end of the year 2000: "The dismantling of the 'insurmountable walls' erected through the centuries between the different Churches has shown itself to demand more time than what was foreseen. The theological differences persist and do not allow themselves to be easily disassociated from the social-cultural factors in which they are inextricably anchored. The notion of 'visible unity,' even though always officially claimed, was affected by the breakdown of the overly idealized image of an 'indivisible' Church that supposedly would have regrouped the first Christians.

*Folha de S. Paulo, Oct. 17, 1995*

On October 12, 1995, the feast day of the patroness of Brazil, Our Lady of Aparecida, Protestant bishop Sergio Von Helder proffered many blasphemies against Our Lady during a televised program. In a manifestation of his hatred, the minister kicked a copy of the sacred statue, as shown in the photo taken from the broadcast and published throughout Brazil. This act raised strong indignation all over the country. The Catholic Episcopate managed to anesthetize the general fury.

This brazen act revealed the arrogance of the Protestants that is hidden behind the smiling mask of ecumenism. The significant spread of Protestant sects in Brazil, still the most Catholic country in the world, is one of the nefarious fruits of ecumenism.

For some years, the evocative slogans of the 'richness of our differences' have replaced those that used to denounce the 'scandal of our divisions.' For many of the faithful, ecumenism has come to be viewed as a kind of obsession. Suddenly, the euphoria of encounters is replaced by a disillusionment. The desire to be together will have to run the risk of being delayed for a long time due to its clash with doctrinal imperatives, which are very difficult to overcome precisely because they deal with different conceptions of the unity of the Church....

"'I pray that the Jubilee will be a promising opportunity for fruitful cooperation in the many areas that unite us; these are unquestionably more numerous than those which divide us.' The least that can be said is that these words of John Paul II in *Tertio millennio adveniente* (1994) never went beyond the stage of good intention .... The year 2000 did not represent a good ecumenical harvest. Fleeting difficulties or symptoms of a turnaround in the tendency? The 21st century will answer the question."[39]

Thus, Holy Father, one sees that the reality of ecumenism and inter-religious dialogue is quite different from what certain Vatican sources interested in pleasing you are claiming. Apparently based on such optimistic sources, you have affirmed in *Ut unum sint*: "The 'universal brotherhood' of Christians has become a firm ecumenical conviction. Consigning to oblivion the excommunications of the past, communities which were once rivals are now in many cases helping one another: Places of worship are sometimes lent out ...."(n. 42a). The facts show that this imagined "universal fraternity" actually does not exist outside the restricted circle of those

---

[39] Geffroy de Turckeim, "Le XXᵉ siècle a été oecuménique," *Actualité des Religions*, January 2001, p. 19.

*O Estado de S. Paulo.* Sept. 30. 1989

*Above*, Protesters in London against Anglican
archbishop Robert Runcie's visit to John Paul II
at the Vatican.
*Below*, the Anglican bishop of Bristol is surrounded
by newly ordained female priests.
Another insurmountable obstacle to the
utopic ecumenical union.

*Newsweek.* March 21. 1994

who promote and participate in ecumenical encounters and a certain set of Catholics who mistake the dream for the reality.

Therefore, the idea that the reform of the Papacy is going to bring about the union of Protestants and Schismatics also does not seem to correspond to reality.

There is a very grave error that is being committed in the assumption that this pan-religious union is a longing of the multitudes. A deeper analysis of the facts shows, however, that they are silently refusing to go along with this utopist dream, and have increasingly seemed to move in the opposite direction.

If we consider only the practical aspect, the result of this ecumenical adventure is tragic: the destruction of the Papacy without having achieved the disputable "pastoral" advantage: the professed union of the religions. The question inevitably arises: Was the attainment of this ecumenical and pan-religious unity ever really expected? Or was this merely the pretext for carrying out what the revolutionaries, the Liberals, the Modernists, and the Progressivists have been desiring for so long a time – the end of the Papal Monarchy?

\* \* \*

*30 Giorni*, May 1988

An Islamic response to Vatican inter-religious dialogue: At a meeting in Khartoum (Sudan) in 1995, the religious heads of 80 Muslim countries met together to launch a "holy war" with the aim of "emptying the Middle East of Christians."

*L'Actualité Relieieuse*, Feb. 15. 1997

*Left*, a radical religious Jew protesting John Paul II's visit to Jerusalem (2000).

*Below*, Yigal Amir, the assassin of prime minister Yitzhak Rabin with a triumphant air. He was considered a hero by many Jews.

*Above,* Rabbi Beni Alon, Amir's mentor, who admitted that his ideas could have influenced the crime.

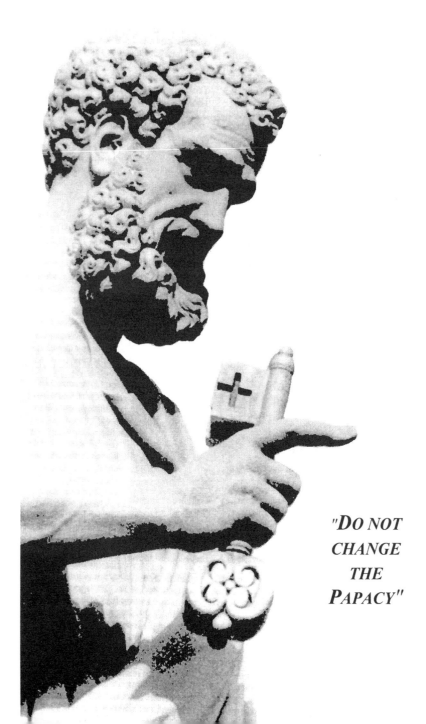

*"DO NOT CHANGE THE PAPACY"*

## Conclusion

Most Holy Father, these are the considerations that we respectfully present to you with the filial request that you answer our appeal. If there is some mistake on our part, we would be grateful for your paternal correction. Could we not hope that you would open a dialogue with the Catholics who do not agree with the change of the Papacy? It seems to us a just request, since you have invited to the discussion table those who for many centuries have vehemently attacked the Petrine Primacy.

We close these lines with our eyes fixed on the horizon, watching for the signs that the Queen of History will give of her announced victory over the Revolution in the Holy Church. We are certain than in the reign of the Immaculate Heart of Mary that will come for the Church and for the world, the Papacy will be restored to its glory of old. Then, attracted by its radiant light, the peoples of the whole world will be drawn to the Catholic Church and will rejoice to have converted to the one true Faith, whose light prefigures the glorious light of the beatific vision. Free from the pollution of their errors and the blindness of their heresies, far from the miry and poisonous waters of syncretism and pan-religion, those who come will be able to contemplate in the crystalline purity of Catholic Doctrine the beauty of all her truths, the image of the Divine Word, Our Lord Jesus Christ. In those fortunate days to come, the need for the Papal Monarchy and Papal Infallibility will be explained as the cornerstones of the Church, society, History, and the whole Universe. These are the glorious days that are approaching – all the more glorious tomorrow as today the steps of the Passion of the Catholic Church are tragic and dolorous. Blessed are those who believe, when almost all turn their backs to the fullness of the Catholic Faith. Yes, blessed, for as the French poet said: "It is at night that it is beautiful to believe in the light."

Thus, asking Our Lady, Seat of Wisdom, to enlighten your mind and strengthen your will so that your actions might best resound for the glory of God, we place at the feet of Your Holiness this urgent and filial plea made with the highest respect for the office with which you are invested and with the highest veneration for the Mystical Body of Christ.

Most Holy Father John Paul II, for the love of the Catholic Faith, for the exaltation of Holy Mother Church, and to deter the revolutionary and progressivist plan of destruction of the Papal Monarchy, we implore you: Do not change the Papacy.

Atila Sinke Guimarães
Author

Michael J. Matt
*The Remnant*, Editor

Marian Therese Horvat, Ph.D
Author and Educator

John Vennari
*Catholic Family News*, Editor

*"We close these lines with our eyes fixed on the horizon, watching for the signs that the Queen of History will give of her announced victory over the Revolution in the Holy Church."*

The four signers of *An Urgent Plea:
Do Not Change the Papacy* met in
April 2001 in Los Angeles.
*From left,* Mr. John Vennari,
Mr. Michael J. Matt, Dr. Marian T.
Horvat, and Mr. Atila Sinke Guimarães.

## RECOMMENDED BY TIA, INC.

*WE RESIST YOU TO THE FACE* – The four authors expose the new doctrines and reforms in the Church since Vatican II, and make a declaration of resistance to those papal teachings "that are objectively opposed to the prior ordinary and extraordinary Magisterium." Includes other articles by the signers and many pictures. 168 pp....$10

*RESISTANCE VS. SEDE-VACANTISM* – Michael Matt and Atila Guimarães respond to critics and explain why the sede-vacantist option is not viable. 20 pp....................................................$4

### WORKS BY ATILA SINKE GUIMARÃES

*IN THE MURKY WATERS OF VATICAN II* – The ambiguity in the official texts of Vatican II opens the door to progressivist interpretations. A classic. Special price – close-out on the 1ST edition. 453 pp...........$15

*ANIMUS DELENDI I* (Desire to Destroy) – Examines the much-discussed *spirit of the Council*. Exposes the plan of self-destruction of the Holy Church by the conciliar progressivists. 502 pp..............$20

*QUO VADIS, PETRE?* (Where are you going, Peter?) – Analyzes the events planned for the Millennium and compares them to perennial Catholic doctrine. Addresses ecumenism. 110 pp. .....................$8

*PETRINE PRIMACY CHALLENGED* – Analysis of three important documents, a lecture and a book by Msgr. John R. Quinn, and a book by Russell Shaw on the reform of the Papacy. 56 pp....................$6

*A CORDIAL INVITATION TO 171 RABBIS AND JEWISH SCHOLARS* – A challenge to Jewish scholars on their recent statement demanding changes in Catholic doctrine. 20pp.........................................$4

*WE ARE CHURCH: RADICAL AIMS, DANGEROUS ERRORS* – A study on the history, aims, methods, and thinking of the progressivist *We Are Church* movement. 32 pp. ...............................................$5

### WORKS BY MARIAN T. HORVAT, PH.D.:

*OUR LADY OF GOOD SUCCESS: PROPHECIES FOR OUR TIMES* – Prophecies that concern our times revealed by Our Lady to a Conceptionist nun in Quito, Ecuador in the 16th century. A 300-year-old approved devotion. A moving and compelling work. 72 pp. .............$7

Turn page

96

## AUDIO CASSETTES BY MARIAN HORVAT – $6 EACH

*OUR LADY OF GOOD SUCCESS: PROPHETIC REVELATIONS* – How the prophecies of Our Lady of Good Success harmonize with – and complete – those of Our Lady of Fatima in 1917.

*THE TRUTH ABOUT THE HOLY INQUISITION* – An objective analysis on the Inquisition's origins, purpose and policies. Reveals the bias of the lies and myths that were generated by the enemies of the Church.

*CATHOLIC PSYCHOLOGY: THE FOUR TEMPERAMENT* – The Catholic way to better understand yourself, your spouse, your children. How to identify and work with the temperament God gave you.

*THE DESTRUCTION OF TRUE CULTURE* – The falseness of today's "multiculturalism" vs. the truth of organic Catholic culture based on the Gospel and fostered by the Church.

*TODAY'S GREAT MYTH: THE TRUTH LIES IN THE CENTER* – Refutes the great lie of our day, that is, the truth lies between the radical poles of good and evil. Sanctity demands radicalism.

*THE REVOLUTION IN CLOTHING* – Men's and women's clothing has suffered from the egalitarian and vulgar spirit of the cultural revolution. How clothes reveal the person.

**Additional copies of *An Urgent Plea: Do Not Change the Papa*cy can be purchased for $7.**

### TO PLACE AN ORDER, USE

- ❖ Our Website: www.traditioninaction.org
- ❖ Our Order-line: 323-725-0219
- ❖ Our Fax: 323-832-9605
- ❖ Our Address: P.O. Box 23135 – Los Angeles, CA 90023

### Please add the Shipping and Handling:

**U.S. orders**: If your total is less than $15, add $3, $15 to $29, add $4; $30 to $49, add $6; $50 to $99, add $7.50; $100 or more, 5%.
**Canadian orders**: Add $3.00 for each order.
**International orders:** Call us or fax us for charges.

## TRADITION IN ACTION, INC.